How To Write A
Screenplay

Jessica Cruz

How To Write A Screenplay
by Jessica Cruz

ISBN 978-1-926917-10-8

Printed in the United States of America

Neither the author nor the publisher assumes
any responsibility for the use or misuse of
information contained in this book.

TABLE OF CONTENTS

Introduction to
Screenwriting

If you have ever had an idea pop into your head that you thought would make a blockbuster film or compelling television show, you may have found yourself wondering where to get the process started. The process of getting a script, whether it is for television or the big screen, on paper is known as screenwriting. While the process of committing your idea to paper might seem simple enough, if you really want to succeed in the world of television and feature films you need to known the precise formula and rules that are used when writing a script.

Isn't writing all about creativity, you might ask? Yes, that is certainly true and without creativity there would likely be no scripts for award winning films and television programs, but like anything else, there are rules and conventions that must be adhered to, especially if your goal is to have your script read by professionals in the industry who really have the power and connections to bring your script to life on screen.

Keep in mind that the real power powers, such as producers and commissioning editors, all receive a ton of scripts on their desk almost on a daily basis and in order to sort through those scripts to separate the gems from the junk they must be able to quickly and easily pick out those that seem to have the potential to be real winners. This means they must be able to quickly pick up those that scream 'newbie' and separate them from the clear professionals. The latter category is where you want your script to fall. Unconventional formatting may seem creative to you, but to the powers that be it simply announces you as someone new to the industry and likely will land your script in the trash without it having even been read. It might well be the greatest script ever written, but keep in mind that if you cannot get it into the right hands, no one will ever know that. Writing to the correct standard and format will immediately give you the best opportunity to have your script read.

In this guide we are going to take a look at some of the standard formatting regulations for writing scripts both for television and film and give you an insider's look at the industry.

Are you ready to find out what it takes to write a successful script?

Let's get started!

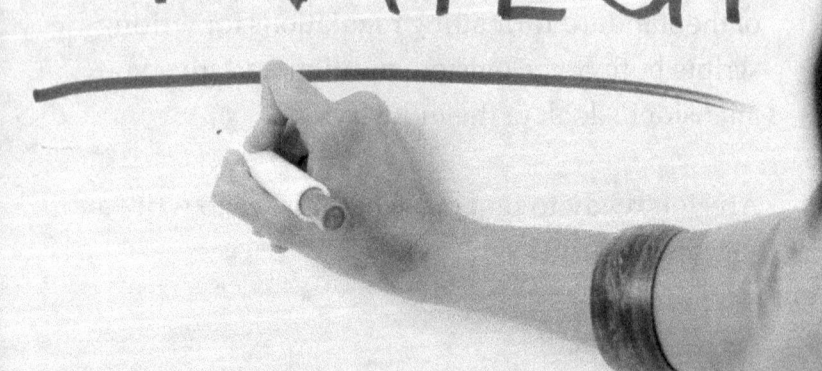

Chapter 1

What's in a Script?

Before we begin to look at the various components of a script and how you actually go about writing a compelling script, it is a good idea to first examine what a script is. Simply put, a script is a document that is used to outline the elements that are needed to tell a story. The key difference between a script and the story itself is that the script is actually a collaboration that involves not only the writer but also the director, editor, cast and various production crew members. There are many people involved in the process of creating television or film and the script that you write must conform to all of the standard conventions including notations, margins, layout and formatting in order for those numerous people to be able to work effectively together.

A script is also different from a novel or any other type of written work in that it is a medium that is visual in nature. With a script, your job is not to tell the story to the audience but rather to show it to them. This means that you must learn to write in a way that is visual so that the audience can see the story come alive. While your character's thoughts may be quite alive inside your own head, you must be able to reveal what they are thinking and show it on screen through their actions. This can sometimes be accomplished with a mere look.

The Right Elements for a Good Story

We all know a good story when we see one on screen. The characters sweep you right along with you, force you to become involved, captivate you with the emotions they portray and leave you wanting more. A good story not only allows the audience to develop an interest in the characters but to become passionate about them. This does not necessarily mean they always like the characters; but it does mean the characters evoke a strong emotional response.

One of the hallmarks of any good story is that there is always something at stake. Whatever it is; whether it is romance, something for the good of mankind or something monetary; whatever it is it must be extremely powerful and the drive to obtain it must be more important than anything else and as the story continues to unfold, the drive to obtain it must become more important and more desperate.

Naturally, there must also be obstacles along the way. The story would not amount to much if the hero or heroine obtained whatever it was they wanted within the first five minutes. There must be conflict. Something or someone is continually getting in the way of whatever the main character is seeking.

You also need to provide a hook to initially gain the interest of the audience. Something that catches their attention. Many writers begin by thinking "what if?" What if such and such happened? If you are able to craft a good enough 'what if' scenario, your script will be able to stand apart from the crowd on its own strength and merits.

Finally, there is the matter of formatting, which is something that we will address in greater depth in a subsequent chapter. The importance of formatting cannot be stressed enough. Your script must look as though it was written by someone with years of experience in the industry. The volume of script submissions received by producers each and every day is nothing if not sheer astounding. If you want to play the game, you must know the rules and you must follow them. To the letter.

Chapter 2

Styles of Scripts

Before we begin looking at the various components that make up a script and the correct formatting procedure for writing a script, it is a good idea to first examine the different types of script formats that are used.

Scriptwriters for television dramas and feature films typically present their work in one of two different styles. The difference usually depends upon whether the work has already been sold and production is in process or whether the scriptwriter is currently trying to sell the work.

Submission Script

A submission script is also frequently known as a spec script. This is a script that is written and which has not been bought or commissioned to date. In other words, it is written on the speculation or hope that it will be purchased.

Shooting Script

Once a script has actually been purchased, it will usually go through a number of rewrites before it ever goes into production. Once it goes into production the script then becomes a production or shooting script. All of the shots and scenes contained inside the shooting script will then be numbered and each scene as well as each shot will be broken down into the number of relevant components that are needed for filming. The director and production assistance can arrange scenes in the order that they will be shot in order to make the most efficient use of the cast, stage and resources for location. This means that scenes are often not shot in the order they will actually appear on screen.

sailing right before the
wind as you will perceive
by the lat & longitude
which through the medium
of our paper I am enabled
to obtain, daily, the skipper
furnishes us with it from
the ships log so it is sure
to be correct. –

Now for our 'Bill of Fare' I
will write it as I find it
in our cabin viz: –

– Notice to Passengers –

– Cooking days –

Sunday . Preserved Beef & Doe
Monday . Pork & Peas
Tuesday . Beef & Rice
Wednesday . Pres. Beef & Potat
Thursday . Beef & Dough
Friday . Pork & Peas
Saturday . Beef & Rice –

Chapter 3

Your Script Layout

One of the biggest mistakes that many people make when they are first starting out writing a script is to put it in the wrong layout. Writing a script is completely different from writing a novel. Yes, they both tell a story, but a script also accomplishes much more than a novel in that it must also provide instructions and direction. Putting your script in the right format is the first step to ensuring that you are taken seriously as a professional screenwriter.

Length and Format

The length of the script is used to determine how long a television episode or film will be. This is extremely important and it is something that producers live and die by. A well written script will allow a producer to immediately know how long the film or television episode should run. Although there can be a small amount of variance the general rule is that one page of script equates to one minute of screen time. Therefore, a script that is written for an hour long television drama is going to run roughly between 45 and 50 pages in length. Why 45 or 50 and not 60? Because the episode does not last exactly sixty minutes. Time must be allowed for commercial breaks. The average 'hour long' television drama really only runs about 43-45 minutes. The same is also true for a 30-minute television program. Only about 23 minutes or so is devoted to actual on screen time.

Obviously, this is somewhat different when you are looking at a feature film for the big screen because there will be no commercial breaks; but the rule remains the same; roughly one page of script for one minute of on screen time. By looking at the length of your script, it should be easily visible how long your film or program will be. Each page of your script should be clearly numbered to assist in this process.

For a feature screenplay, the traditional script length is between 95 and 125 pages. Most scripts usually will not run longer than an average of 114 pages. If it is a comedy, the script tends to be longer while dramatic scripts tend to be somewhat longer. Of course, there are exceptions to every rule. A film that is full of action might actually be shorter in terms of script length but take much longer in regards to film time.

The length of the script is extremely important. When a script is turned in to a producer, the first thing the producer is likely to do is to turn to the last page to see how long it is. It will not matter if you have the best story ever written; if it's too long, the producer is likely to refuse to look at it any further.

Economic considerations generally drive the dislike for longer scripts in the industry. When a film is less than two hours, more showings can be held in a day in the theater; which means there is more revenue potential for the theater as well as the distributor and the filmmaker.

125 pages are considered to be on the long side for a script. If you see that your script is proving to be too lengthy and that you will need to start paring it down, remember that if you can remove a scene and the story still works, that scene was never essential to the story anyway. You should only have scenes in your script that are essential to the story. Every scene should serve a purpose; to move the story along to its conclusion.

Formatting

Now that we understand the importance of the length of the script, we need to address a few other important areas, such as how the script should be formatted in terms of font, margins, spacing, etc.

In most instances screenplays are written on 8 ½"
x 11" white paper that is 3-hole punched.

Font

The standard font to use for a script is Courier
size 12. The reason this font is used is for the
purposes of timing. One page of script in Courier
12 averages the 1 minute of on screen time that is
needed.

Page Numbers

The page number should be positioned in the
upper right hand corner.

Margins

The top and bottom page margins should be
between .5" and 1". The left margin should be
between 1.2" and 1.6". The right page margin
should be between .5" and 1". This will leave an
additional inch of white space on the left of the
script page to allow it to be bound using brads.

The Elements of the Script

There are several elements that make up a script,
which you will need to be aware of. They are:

- Scene heading
- Action
- Character name
- Dialogue
- Parenthetical
- Extensions
- Transition
- Shot

Scene Headings

Scene headings, also known as slug lines, are always aligned flush left approximately 1.5" from the edge of the paper. They will usually not be so long as to reach the right page margin. The scene heading is always written using all CAPS. There are two types of scene headings; location and time.

The purpose of the scene heading is to let the reader know where a particular scene takes place. For example, does it occur indoors or outdoors? The name of the location is also usually included; such as OFFICE, CAR, LIVING ROOM, etc. In addition the scene heading might also include other information such as the time of day to help set the scene.

Scene Headings-Location

INT/EXT: These headings refer to the location of the scene. If the scene is to take place inside, then you would have INT for interior or likewise EXT for exterior. This will be immediately followed by the precise location. A period should always be used after either INT. or EXT. A hyphen should be used between any other elements of the scene heading.

Scene Headings-Time

DAY/NIGHT: These headings refer to whether the scene takes place during the day or at night. This will immediately follow the direction. Keep in mind that you should never substitute words such as morning or evening. Stick with day or night.

In some cases a scene heading might also include some production information such as ESTABLISHING SHOT, CONTINUOUS ACTION OR STOCK SHOT. Some examples of how scene headings might be used include:

INT. LIVING ROOM-EVENING
EXT.BEACH-SUNSET
INT.LOS ANGELES FREEWAY-MORNING-ESTABLISHING

EXT.NEW YORK CITY-MACY'S PARADE-STOCK FOOTAGE

If you are using scriptwriting software, the software will automatically file each new scene heading that you create. This will remove the need to retype the same heading over and over and also ensure that your script remains consistent. Consistency between scene headings ensures that the reader will be able to more easily recognize locations and places and not have to try to determine whether a new scene is being introduced.

Here is an example of how a scene heading might appear in script form:

FADE IN:
INT.LOS ANGELES FREEWAY-MORNING-ESTABLISHING

This establishes that the scene takes place on Los Angeles freeway in the morning.

Action

Action always runs from the left margin to the right margin, taking the full width of the page. You should be sure that you have selected the word wrap tool or function in whatever program or software you are using to ensure that editing and rewrites are as easy as possible. Text should be single-spaced and in mixed case rather than all caps. When using script writing software, it will usually automatically format the spacing and text between paragraph styles for you. The action will set the scene as well as describe the setting while you introduce characters.

Remember that action is always written in real time as opposed to the past tense. Everything takes place right now, in the present. You should use active voice, not passive voice. For example: a door slams close. Not; a door is slammed close.

Paragraphs should be kept short. They should never ramble and should not extend beyond five lines at the most.

Example:

FADE IN:
INT.LOS ANGELES FREEWAY-MORNING-ESTABLISHING

Bumper to bumper traffic fills the freeway in the early morning sunlight.

INT. CAR-MORNING

Sunlight filters through the windows of an expensive foreign car. DEVON REYNOLDS, 34, handsome and dressed in a designer suit, adjusts the radio dial.

This description allows the reader to immediately begin forming an idea about the setting as well as what is currently taking place in this scene. The reader knows that the scene occurs inside a car; that the car is expensive and foreign and a character has been introduced. The reader also knows that the character is in his mid-30's and good looking. When writing the description of the action taking place in the scene, you should try to avoid including any camera shots and angles. This cannot always be completely avoided, but whenever possible you should strive to steer clear of it.

Remember; you are the writer, not the director. Some common directing terms include "widen shot", "cut to" and "pan across." The only time such terms should be used in the script is when movement within the script could not be understood without the use of such terms. These terms are generally only used on the shooting script; the final script. While you may see these terms used in a professional script if you obtained a copy of one, this is not how you should write a script to be pitched to a producer.

The Introduction of Characters

The first time that a character will make an appearance in your script, you will need to be sure that the character name is written in all CAPS. This will be immediately followed by a description of the character that provides a first impression. You do not need to go into a tremendous amount of detail here, but provide enough information that the script reader can immediately gain a sense of this character. Such as GWEN: a middle-aged housewife lacking in self-confidence. That tells you much more than if you had just written GWEN: 45, mousy brown hair and slightly overweight.

Keep in mind at this point that you do not need to provide any acting directions in the dialogue. Your job is to make the emotions clear from the context of the dialogue, not to tell the actors who will eventually portray your characters how to do so.

Character's Names

The character name should be written in all CAPS and should be indented 3.5" from the left margin. The character name should always precede any dialogue from the character so the reader knows who is speaking. In many cases the character name will be an actual name, like (JACK) or it could be a description should as (FLIGHT ATTENDANT). If there is one more than character with the same description you might have something like FLIGHT ATTENDANT #1 AND FLIGHT ATTENDANT #2.

If you use script writing software, the program will automatically learn and then keep track of any character names that you use, which makes it much easier to remain consistent in your script. The software will also ensure that the correct spacing is used.

Example:

FADE IN:
INT.LOS ANGELES FREEWAY-MORNING-ESTABLISHING

Bumper to bumper traffic fills the freeway in the early morning sunlight.

INT. CAR-MORNING

Sunlight filters through the windows of an expensive foreign car. DEVON REYNOLDS, 34, handsome and dressed in a designer suit, adjusts the radio dial.

DEVON

Dialogue

Dialogue should always be indented 2.5" from the left margin. A line of dialogue may from between 30 spaces and 35 spaces in length; which means that the right margin can be somewhat flexible; ranging between 2.0" and 2.5".

Anytime that someone on screen speaks, the rules of dialogue apply. The dialogue you use in your script should always sound conversational and natural. The reader should feel as though they are actually hearing the characters peak. Most script writers will find it to be a good idea to read dialogue aloud to hear how it actually sounds. If a line sounds stilted or unnatural when you read it aloud, it will probably sound the same on screen.

Example:

FADE IN:

INT.LOS ANGELES FREEWAY-MORNING-ESTABLISHING

Bumper to bumper traffic fills the freeway in the early morning sunlight.

INT. CAR-MORNING
Sunlight filters through the windows of an expensive foreign car. DEVON REYNOLDS, 34, handsome and dressed in a designer suit, adjusts the radio dial.

                    DEVON

Great. Temperatures in the high 90s. Another scorching day in L.A.

Parenthetical

Parenthicals are indented to the left at 3.0" with a right margin of approximately 3.5"; although there is some flexibility allowed. Parentheticals should not be centered beneath the name of the character. A parenthetical remark can be used as a verbal direction or even an action that should be taken by the actor who is speaking that part. In some cases it could be used to reflect an attitude.

Anytime a parenthetical is used it should be to the point and short. You should also only use a parenthetical when it is absolutely necessary. Remember that as the scriptwriter, it is not your job to provide direction to the actors or director.

An example of a parenthetical would be:

DEVON
(sarcastically)
Great. Another lovely day in L.A.

In some instances a parenthetical might also be used in a script as a type of continuing notation. For instance, if a character is speaking and that dialogue is followed by an action line and then the same characters continues their dialogue, a notation might be used.

Example:

DEVON
(sarcastically)
Great. Another lovely day in L.A.

Devon changes the radio station. He listens for a moment to a talk show and then changes the radio again to a rock station.

> DEVON
> (continuing)
> That's more like it.

If you use a script writing program, the program may give you the choice of being able to place the (continuing) as a parenthetical remark or you may be able to place it with the same like as the character name so that it appears as an extension.

Example:

> DEVON
> (sarcastically)
> Great. Another lovely day in L.A.

Devon changes the radio station. He listens for a moment to a talk show and then changes the radio again to a rock station.

> DEVON (CONT'D)
> That's more like it.

Extensions

An extension is a technical note that is to be placed directly to the right of the character name to note the way the character's name will be heard by the audience. For example off-screen or voice over. An off-screen voice might be heard from a character that is in another room or just out of camera range. Off screen extensions are noted as (O.S.).

Example:

DEVON
Pushes the speed dial on his cell phone.

RECEPTIONIST (O.S.)
Reynolds and Associates. How may I help you?

In some cases a writer might use O.C. to refer to off-camera instead of O.S.

If the character needs to pause in their dialogue, the term beat is used.

Example:

DEVON
Pushes the speed dial on his cell phone.

RECEPTIONIST (O.S.)
Burns and Associates. How may I help you?

DEVON

This is Devon Reynolds. I need to speak to Mr. Burns.

(beat)

We have a ten o'clock appointment.

When a character needs to narrate or speak when they are not actually in the scene, the voice over or V.O. direction might be used. When a voice over is used, the dialogue is recorded and then will be laid over the scene in the editing process.

Example:

DEVON (V.O.)

I had a hunch my day was about to go downhill when that perky receptionist said my appointment had been canceled.

Formatting the First and Last Pages of your Script

The First Page of your Script

Now, the exciting part. The first words of your script, no matter what the plot or the genre should be "FADE IN." Please note that this is really not any type of instruction for the director but is simply an international custom that is commonly used for beginning a script.

The Last Page of your Script

The last page of your script should conclude with The End, centered and double spaced to the far right. You should then have "FADE OUT." Once again, this is not a directorial instruction, but simply a customary way of ending professional scripts.

Scene Numbering

It is also important that you do not number the scenes. The pages should be numbered but the scenes should not at this point. Scenes are only actually numbered when the final 'shooting script' is ready to go. Why? It is not uncommon for scenes to be moved around within a script up until that final shooting script is ready to go, so it would really be pointless to number them until then.

Chapter 4

Shots

Shots are formatted in a manner that is similar to a scene heading; which means that they have a flush left margin and are written in all CAPS. There is always a blank line before and after a shot.

Shots are used to tell a reader that the focal point within a scene has now changed. Some common examples of shots include:

- ANGLE ON
- EXTREME CLOSE UP
- DEVON'S POV
- PAN TO
- REVERSE ANGLE

You should only use a shot when it is absolutely necessary to redirect the focus of the reader. If you use shots more frequently there is the risk of interrupting the flow of the story. Remember, your job is not to direct the story but to write it.

In some cases a shot may be truly necessary. For instance, you may feel that the reader needs to see something that would not be otherwise obvious within the scene. A shot allows you to do that.

Example:

DEVON
And to make matters even better,
it's bumper to bumper traffic today.

ANGLE ON - A BLUE CONVERTIBLE ZIPS AHEAD OF DEVON'S CAR.

An insert shot may also be used in some cases. A insert shot is only used as a direction in order to focus on something that is critical to the scene. In most cases, it will be used to focus on something that the audience must see that would be too small to be clearly seen in a scene that is full and wide.

Example:

INSERT-DEAR JOHN LETTER

Like most shots, you should only use an insert shot when it is absolutely necessary. If you have an action paragraph that is well constructed you may be able to reach the same goal without the need to distract the reader.

Page Breaks

When you need to end a page, keep in mind that you should never end a page using a scene heading unless you have a shot or another scene heading immediately following; such as an establishing shot and an interior shot.

You should also never start a page using a transition or end a page by using a character name line. Make sure you have a minimum of two lines of dialogue if there is more than one. In addition, be sure that you never end a page using a parenthetical. You should always make sure dialogue follows. If you have dialogue and then a parenthetical and then more dialogue, be sure to break the page before the parenthetical.

This process can be much easier with script writing software because it will usually automatically handle all of this for you.

Adding Finer Touches

The above rules will help you to write a script that is industry standard acceptable. By following these rules your script will appear to be professionally written and no one will automatically assume that you are a novice or amateur script writer. With that said, there are a few finer touches that you can use to really give your script the mark of a honed professional.

Dual Dialogue

Dual dialogue is also sometimes known as side-by-side dialogue. This element can be used when two characters speak at the same time.

Example:

DEVON
How could you let this happen?
Are you stupid?

CHARLES
This is not my fault! Don't blame me!
You're the one who forgot to confirm the appointment!

This is not a technique that you would normally use often but it can be utilized if characters must speak simultaneously.

Adlibs

In some instances you may need to have ad lib dialogue. This often occurs within a crowd scene. There are two ways that this can be done. An action line is one way to handle this.

Example:

The CROWD surrounding the accident scene questions the POLICE OFFICER: "What's going on?" "Why isn't the traffic moving?" "How long is this gonna take?"

The second option is to use a character and dialogue.

Example:

CROWD
What's going on? Why isn't the traffic moving? How long is this gonna take?

Montage

A montage is a type of device that is used to demonstrate a series of scenes; all of which are related and are used to build to a conclusion. It is primarily used to reveal a passage of time.

Example:

MONTAGE:

1) Devon sees Kelly on the sidewalk outside his office and the two embrace.
2) Devon and Kelly enjoy a romantic candlelit dinner.

3) Devon proposes to Kelly in the park on a sunny day.
4) Devon watches Kelly as she walks down the aisle in a beautiful white wedding dress.

These same scenes could also be numbered rather than lettered. As you can see, these scenes are used to demonstrate what occurs over a period of time in a much shorter amount of screen time.

Intercuts

In some instances, you might find it necessary to switch back and forth between multiple scenes. Usually, the scenes occur at the same time. Rather than repeating the same scene heading over and over, you can use an intercut. The intercut provides the reader with a sense that the scene is quickly moving back and forth between different locations.

Example:

INT. DEVON'S APARTMENT-MORNING
Devon buttons his suit jacket and quickly walks toward the door. He turns back around and rushes back to the coffee table and quickly stuffs an item into his pocket.

INT. KELLY'S APARTMENT-MORNING

Kelly hurries toward the door and turns the knob. She hesitates and hurries back to the kitchen to grab a picnic hamper.

INTERCUT BETWEEN DEVON AND KELLY

Devon and Kelly hurry out their apartment doors, both glancing at their watches.

There is also another type of intercut that you can use when two characters are on the phone and you do not wish to have half of the conversation remain off-screen or O.S. and wish to show both characters.

INT. DEVON'S APARTMENT-MORNING

Devon pours a cup of coffee and opens the newspaper.

INT. KELLY'S APARTMENT-MORNING

Kelli picks up her telephone and dials a number.

INTERCUT BETWEEN DEVON AND KELLY

Devon's telephone rings and he answers it.

> DEVON
> Hello, beautiful.

> KELLY
> Is that how you answer all of your calls?

> DEVON
> Only when I know it's a beautiful woman on the other end of the line

A split screen was commonly used in older films in order to demonstrate this type of conversation. This technique is not used quite as commonly today and instead an intercut is usually the best option.

Series of Shots

A series of shots is similar to a montage, but the difference is that a series of shots typically occur in a single location and will be related to the same action.

Example:

SERIES OF SHOTS

   A) Traffic speeds along the freeway.
   B) A blue convertible suddenly veers to the right.
   C) A red mini-van brakes hard and skids into a green truck.
   D) Vehicles begin to slam into one another.

A series of shots is always formatted as a single shot. Just as with a montage, the series of shots are action paragraphs and could also be numbered rather than lettered. Another way to handle a series of shots is to insert them into the script without even noting it as a series of shots.

The reason for doing this is usually to accomplish a smoother flow of action. Action lines are commonly short and descriptive and are placed on separate lines in this case.
Example:

Pacific Palisades is packed with early morning, bumper to bumper traffic.

A blue convertible suddenly veers to the right, causing a LOUD CRASH.

A red mini-van brakes hard, TIRES SQUEAL, and skids into a green truck.

HORNS BLARE. Vehicles begin to slam into one another.

Handling Short Lines, Poetry and Song Lyrics

In some instances, you may need to write dialogue using a series of short lines. For example, if you have a character that is singing or reciting poetry.

Example:

DEVON

Roses are red,

Violets are blue,

I'm in love

Do you feel that too?

When song lyrics are used, they are usually written in all CAPS.

KELLY

(singing)

HAPPY BIRTHDAY TO YOU!

HAPPY BIRTHDAY TO YOU!

HAPPY BIRTHDAY DEAR DEVON!

HAPPY BIRTHDAY TO YOU!

LABS
RAYS
NEEDLES
KBS
BTS
HYPOS

Chapter 5

Abbreviations

There are several abbreviations that are commonly used in scriptwriting as a type of shortcut within a script. While you do not necessarily need to use such shortcuts, you may find that it saves some time. We have already introduced several common shortcuts, such as O.S., V.O. and O.C.

Others include:

B.G.-Background; used in an action paragraph.

Example:
Devon stared out the window. In the b.g., Kelly is preparing dinner.

CGI-Computer generated image; used to note action that would not be able to be normally filled and will require the use of computers to generate the imagery.

F.G.-Foreground; commonly used in action much in the same way as b.g. with the exception that the action occurs in the foreground.

SFX-sound effects; used to let the sound crew know when an effect is needed.
SFX: The BLAST of a car horn

SPFX- special effects; notes when a special effect is required.

M.O.S.-without sound

POV-point of view; used to note when the camera will 'see' the action from the position of a specific character.

NEW
EXPERIMENTS
PHYSICO-MECHANICAL,

Touching

The SPRING of the AIR, and its EFFECTS,

Made, for the moſt part, in a New

Pnuematical Engine,

Written by way of LETTER

To the Right Honorable *CHARLES* Lord

Vicount of *DUNGARVAN,*

Eldeſt Son to the EARL of *CORKE.*

By the Honorable *ROBERT BOYLE* Eſq;

LONDON,

Printed by *Miles Fleſher* for *Richard Davis,* Bookſeller in
Oxford, MDCLXXXII.

Chapter 6

Titles and Opening Credits

When writing a spec script, you usually will not need to worry about inserting beginning and ending titles and credits because it can be difficult to determine where the director and producer will want to insert the titles and where the opening credits should roll.

If you absolutely must use titles and credits, they can be handled in the following manners:

Superimposing a Title

When you wish to place text on top of film footage you use a superimose or title over. This will usually only be used if the director believes there is information the audience needs to know; such as the timing of the next scene or the place.

Example:

EXT. CENTRAL PARK-DAY

Dozens of people are scattered around the park. SUPERIMPOSE: Central Park, Summer, 2010 Only the text "Central Park, Summer, 2010" will appear on the bottom of the screen.
You should generally refrain from superimposing unless you absolutely must use it to depart necessary information to the audience.

Title Page

The title page will contain very specific information. This information should be types using the same font as the script; Courier 12. You do not need special paper or graphics. The only information that should be contained on the title page includes:

The title of the script-centered vertically and horizontally on the page in bold type.

Written by -two lines below, centered.

Your Name-two lines below, centered.

Your contact info, including agent-lower right hand corner

Registered, WGA or copyright notification-lower left hand corner.

Example:

The Banker's Dilemma
Written by - John Doe

Copyright © 2010 by John Doe   John Doe
Registered, WGAw   1234 Main St.
                                      Anytown,
                        CA 12345 (310) 555-1212

TV Movie Title Pages

In a TV movie format, the title of the script, the show and the episode is usually placed at the top on the first page. You can use either mixed case or uppercase.

The title should be placed in quotation marks.

The text should be centered on the line.

The words Fade In will follow the act title.

Example:

"The Banker's Dilemma"
<u>ACT ONE</u>

FADE IN:

INT. BANK LOBBY - MORNING

You will use the words FADE OUT to note the end of each act.

Example:

FADE OUT.

END OF ACT ONE

ACT TWO

FADE IN:

If you are using a scriptwriting software you should make a note to place a forced page break in between acts so that the new act will begin at the top of a new page.

Remember, you do not need to number the scenes at this point. The production office will handle that.

A movie of the week might also include a cast list and a set list on a separate sheet; but that is not always the case. This is a trend that tends to change from time to time within the industry.

noh mal wieder komm.
Noch habe ich eine Bitte an
an euch Geld habt ihr wie
Mist Kauf euch ein Radio
und wenn ihr ein Kauft
dann kauf euch was guts
den abi. Mist da is das Geld
umsonst weggeschmissen, und
wenns euch schade um Geld
ist da kauft euch für mein
Geld ein 170 hab ich schon geschikt
und wen ich noch 170 Mark schicke
dann gibts ein Ent klassigen
Aparat, Ohne Radio ist man
dummer mensch in Reich
hat jeder Arbeiter ein Radio.
Noch eins ihr habt mir geschrie=
ben der Tim baut euch das
Haus an laßt euch nicht

Chapter 7

Production Drafts

So, what happens after you have sold your script? Time to move on to the next phase and that is the production draft and revisions. There are a few key differences between production drafts and spec scripts that you should be aware of and one of the main differences is numbered scenes. Previously we mentioned that in a spec script scenes are not usually numbered. They are in a production draft. The good news is that a script writing program can automatically handle this for you by numbering the scene headings with numbers to the left and right of the scene heading. The idea behind this is to help the producer and assistant director in breaking down the scenes for scheduling and budgeting purposes.

Example:

REVISED April 30, 2010 BLUE   1.

FADE IN:

1   EXT. LOS ANGELES FREEWAY -
           MORNING - ESTABLISHING
1

Bumper to bumper traffic fills the freeway.

Locking Script Pages

Once the script has been 'published' and has been given to the department heads and actors, it is essential for the pages to be locked so that in the even there are any changes made following this, they can be tracked easily. If there are any changes to be made to the script after it has been circulated, only revised pages will be printed and then distributed. Revised pages must be easily included in the script without re-arranging any of the original pages. Generally, once a script is locked, if more material is added than will fit on that page, a script writing program will generate an "A" page and any subsequent writing will include a "B" page. For example, Page 115A or Page 115B.

Locking Scenes

Scene numbers must also remain the same in a published script. For example if a scene is omitted, while the number is retired, it will remain in the script and will have the word OMITTED next to it. If a new scene is added it must have a letter positioned next to the number to show where it was added after the original scenes have been locked. A script writing program will usually generate an "A" scene number automatically if a scene is added to the script. Also, any revisions will be automatically generated in a scriptwriting program and then marked with an asterisk in the right margin.

Example:

1 OMITTED   1*

2 INT. CAR - MORNING   2

Sunlight filters through the windows of an expensive foreign car. DEVON REYNOLDS, 34, handsome and dressed in a designer suit, adjusts the radio dial.

2A INT. KITCHEN - MORNING   2A*

DEVON pours a cup of coffee and opens the newspaper. The telephone RINGS and he hurries to answer it.

Headers

A header is another element that is used in the production draft. It resides in the same space as the page number; on the right and .5" from the top of the page. Every script page contains header information including the date of the revision and the color of the page.

Example:

REVISED July 10, 2010 YELLOW   1.

This header will print at the top of every revised page when using a scriptwriting program until you choose to omit it on the first page. It should also be included on the first page of a production draft.

Other Script Formats

Up to this point we have primarily discussed spec scripts. There are other script formats in which the same elements are used, including:

- Movie of the Week
- Hour Episodic Television Shows
- Direct TV Movies

You will find that the formats that are used in these types of scripts are almost exactly the same as that which is used in a spec script. The main difference is that in these types of screenplays, the script is broken down into acts that are then delineated within the body of the script. An act covers the portion of the story that occurs in between commercials. So, basically an act break is really a commercial break.

For example, when this type of scripts begins, it starts with:

ACT ONE

When a particular act ends, you would note it as:

END OF ACT ONE

A movie of the week script will usually have seven acts. It will end with:

THE END

A movie of the week will usually have a "teaser" that is three to eight minutes that starts the story and begins with:

TEASER

Teasers are not end with END OF TEASER. Instead, the scene will simply end and you will begin a new page where Act One begins.

With a one-hour episodic television script, there will usually also be a teaser, although it is typically shorter than one used in a movie. A movie of the week will also commonly have a "Tag" scene that is at the end in order to finish off the story.

The number of acts contained in a one-hour episodic television script will usually have four acts; but that can vary according to specific shows. Both forms use continuous page numbering.

Chapter 8

Screenwriting Software

If the idea of formatting your first script sounds somewhat daunting on your own, you might consider the use of screenwriting software. This type of software is specifically designed to help you ensure your script is in the correct format. There are many different types of screenwriting software programs available. Some programs are actually standalone applications that can be used right on your desktop while others are web applications that are designed to run inside a web browser so that you do not have to worry about installing any type of software.

The latter type of application utilizes a personal log-in. In addition, there are also some applications that are available which can be used as an add-in for a word processing program like Microsoft Word. Along with the basic formatting, some screenwriting programs also include budgeting, production and collaborative editing tools.

Some of the more common screenwriting programs that are available today include:

Page 2 Stage
This is a Windows platform program that is designed to be used for writing scripts, plays

and screen plays. It is available in 30 different languages.
www.page2stage.com

Script Buddy

This is an Internet app platform program, meaning it is completely web based. To use the program you will need to sign up for an account with ScriptBuddy. All of your scripts will be stored in your personal account so that they cannot be accessed by anyone else.
www.scriptbuddy.com

ScriptTeX

This is a free macro program that is available to format scripts, including screenplays.
www.aidtopia.com/software/scripttex

Zhura

This is another web based application that is available for writing and formatting screenplays. It offers a collaborative tools that make it possible to work together in public or in private groups.
www.zhura.com

Scripped

This is an Internet based application that offers script registration as well as script writing.

http://scripped.com

The above screenwriting programs are generally available for free, or at least offer a demo or trial version. The programs below are available for purchase.

Script Wizard

This is a Windows based program that offers full service script writing add on capabilities for Word. Tools include page break, format, writing, editing, scene numbering, proofing, print and even the ability to deliver scripts via email or fax.

www.warrenassoc.com

Final Draft

This program is available for both Mac and Windows and is designed for writing television episodes, stage plays and movie scripts.

www.finaldraft.com

Movie Magic Screenwriter

This program is available for Mac and automates certain formatting elements such as action, dialogue, character, etc.

www.screenplay.com

Movie Outline

This program is available for Mac and Windows and offers an intuitive design based on step-outlining, making it possible to format a screenplay scene by scene.

www.movieoutline.com

Montage

This program is available for Mac OS X and offers editing, creation and screenplay management. It allows you to import Final Draft documents and includes templates for film, television and theater that are custom and pre-formatted.

www.marinersoftware.com

DreamaScript

This program is available for Windows and Mac.

www.dreamascript.com

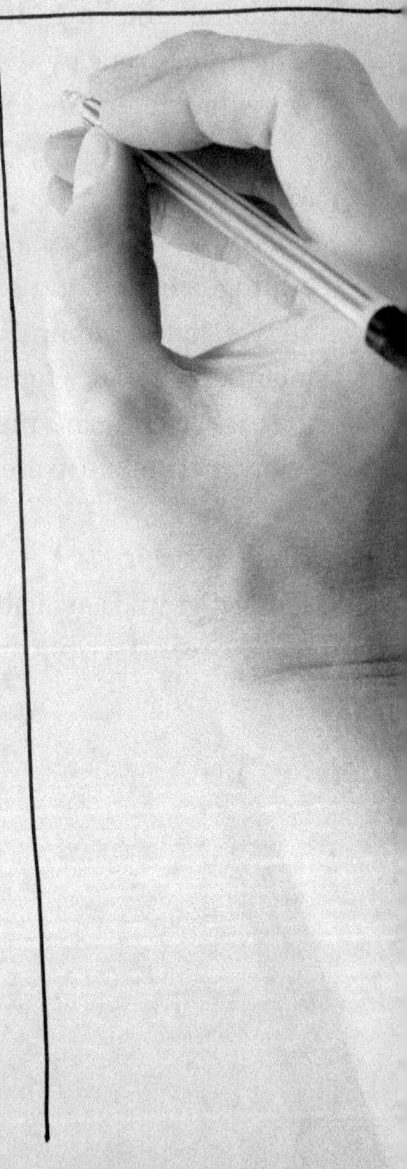

PRO's	CON's

Final Do's and Don'ts

Do's

- Always make sure you proofread your script before submitting it; preferably twice. Spelling and grammar are extremely important. Do not make the mistake of relying on your spell check program as it could easily miss grammatical errors and some terms will not be built-into the dictionary.

- Ask someone else to proofread your script. They may catch something you missed.

- Use high quality brass brads for binding your script. Acco #5 brads are the best quality because they generally have enough length to fit through the entire thickness of the script. Be sure to use solid brass brads and not brass-plated brads.

- Make sure you register your script with the Writers Guild of America and copyright it. The WGA registration will expire somewhat quickly, but a copyright will last for many years.

- Always send a one page cover letter along with your script when you submit it. The letter should be concise, short and to the point; detailing what the script is about and where you can be reached.

Don'ts

- Never create a title page that is fancy and makes use of colored letters, huge fonts, etc. The title page should have the title, the name of the screenwriter(s) and contact information placed in the lower right hand corner.

- Never place a date on the script or the version of your draft.

- Never place blank pages in the script.

- Never place a quote on the title page.

- Never include a back story of a page with character descriptions. While this may be customary in some cases in the theater industry, it is not a convention that is used in the film industry. Your story should tell anything that needs to be known.

- Never place the script title on the first page.

- Never use anything other than 20# 3-hole punch paper.

- Never use colored paper. Color paper is only used for production scripts. Never use more than two brads; but always make sure you have 3-hole paper. The brads should be placed in the top and bottom holes.

- Never include illustrations.

Conclusion

Hopefully this guide will have given you some insight into the correct and proper way to write and format a script. While there is much to learn about the screenwriting industry and even veteran screenwriters will tell you that it takes time to hone the craft of screenwriting; there is certainly no better way to get started than to simply begin writing. With the guidelines and tips contained in this guide you should be off to a good start!

To your Success!

Other books by Psylon Press:

100% Blonde Jokes
R. Cristi
ISBN 978-0-9866004-1-8

Choosing a Dog Breed Guide
Eric Nolah
ISBN 978-0-9866004-5-6

Best Pictures Of Paris
Christian Radulescu
ISBN 978-0-9866004-8-7

Best Gift Ideas For Women
Taylor Timms
ISBN 978-0-9866004-4-9

Top Bikini Pictures
Taylor Timms
ISBN 978-0-9866426-3-0

Cross Tattoos
Johnny Karp
ISBN 978-0-9866426-4-7

Metal Detecting Tips
Johnny Karp
ISBN 978-0-9866426-2-3

For more books please visit:

www.psylonpress.com